a pocketful of

RH

Imagination fo

2006 Poetry Competition for 7-11 year-olds

Young**Writers**

Inspirations From Essex Vol I
Edited by Donna Samworth

 Young**Writers**

First published in Great Britain in 2006 by:
Young Writers
Remus House
Coltsfoot Drive
Peterborough
PE2 9JX
Telephone: 01733 890066
Website: www.youngwriters.co.uk

SB ISBN 1 84602 569 9

Foreword

Young Writers was established in 1991 and has been passionately devoted to the promotion of reading and writing in children and young adults ever since. The quest continues today. Young Writers remains as committed to the nurturing of poetic and literary talent as ever.

This year's Young Writers competition has proven as vibrant and dynamic as ever and we are delighted to present a showcase of the best poetry from across the UK and in some cases overseas. Each poem has been selected from a wealth of *A Pocketful Of Rhyme* entries before ultimately being published in this, our fourteenth primary school poetry series.

Once again, we have been supremely impressed by the overall quality of the entries we have received. The imagination, energy and creativity which has gone into each young writer's entry made choosing the poems a challenging and often difficult but ultimately hugely rewarding task - the general high standard of the work submitted ensured this opportunity to bring their poetry to a larger appreciative audience.

We sincerely hope you are pleased with this final collection and that you will enjoy *A Pocketful Of Rhyme Inspirations From Essex Vol I* for many years to come.

Contents

Jazmin Mitchell-Blake (8)   80
Ellessi Ricketts (11)   81
Nadeem Mer (8)   82
Amritral Singh Bhogal (8)   83
Filipe Santos (8)   84
Samira Ahmed (7)   85
Ulfet Enver (8)   86
Sofia dos Santos (8)   87
Ameer Hamzah (7)   88
Sanah Mansoor (7)   89
Simran Lotay (7)   90

Hadleigh Junior School
Elouise Atkins (10)   91
Daniel Allen (10)   92
Cameron Heath (10)   93
Liam Conley (9)   94
Alec Waymark (10)   95
Montana Clarke (10)   96
Steven Potter (10)   97
Ellie-Jade Smith (11)   98
Anna Goldup (10)   99
Ella Glazier (10)   100
Jodie Purser (7)   101
Ben Aldridge (8)   102
Lucy Berry (8)   103
Sophie Poyser (9)   104
Niall Manning (8)   105
Samuel Charman & Charlotte Crudgington (8)   106
Frankie Bird (8)   107
Rhys Watson (9)   108
Leigh-Marie Hobday (10)   109

Hamilton Primary School
Tara Pomery (8)   110
Sian King (8)   111
Lily Morgan (7)   112
Melissa Armstrong (8)   113

Hare Street Junior School

Alex Galloni (10)	114
Chelsey Compton (10)	115
Conor Harrison-Luby (10)	116
Ross Squires (10)	117
Saleem Mohammad (10)	118
Marjorie Sunday (10)	119
Bradley Perry (10)	120
Jack Campbell (10)	121
Alice Cracknell (10)	122
Danielle Fry (10)	123
Louise Orme (10)	124
Chusdey Bravo (10)	125
Trina Brown (8)	126
Megan Preston (7)	127
Jack Parker (8)	128
Tatenda Mapanda (10)	129
Chantal Collier (11)	130
Lindiwe Sikabe (10)	131
Natalie Smyth (11)	132
Ashley Clark (11)	133
Jahid Abdul & Sophie-Leigh Dangerfield (8)	134
Macie Harwood-Turner & Jone McKeever (8)	135
Mason King (10)	136
Elen McKeever (10)	137
Aileen O'Reilly (11)	138
Jaidene Neal (11)	139
Jake Budd (11)	140
Reece Nelson (10)	141
Sophie Vanderhoven (10)	142
Bilal-Ben Sghaier (11)	143
Danny Lowles (11)	144
Jordan Gregg (10)	145
Shannon Lockhart (10)	146
Reece Poulter (9)	147
Charlie Burford (8)	148
Sharan Chandran (8)	149
Samina Abdul (9)	150
Jayde Perry (8)	151
Travis Prudence (9)	152
Aylis Emek (8)	153

Manford Primary School

Charlotte Taylor (9)	154
Harry Savage (9)	155
Shani-Maia Anderson (9)	156
Hami Hossain (9)	157
Safia Ewers (9)	158
Alfie Smith (9)	159
Gabriella Long (9)	160
Jessie Allen (9)	161
Odean Johnson (9)	162
Shaun McFarlane (9)	163
Alexandra Elliott (9)	164
Rawal Butt (9)	165
Lareb Khan (8)	166
Milanda Khan (8)	167
Louise Ambrose (9)	168
Heather Everingham (9)	169
Isha Kulkarni (9)	170
Tommy Edwards (9)	171
Neha Karthikeyan (9)	172
Anna Clare (9)	173
Jordan Harry (9)	174
Amie Daniels Lydon (9)	175
Tarrell Hinds (9)	176
Melissa Clare (9)	177

Purleigh Primary School

Jesse Banister Wells (10)	178
Danielle Carruthers (11)	179
Taylor Burne (11)	180
Georgie Gefaell (11)	181
George Dixon (11)	182
Tyler Minot (11)	183
Catherine Harvey (11)	184
Clarke Minot (11)	185
Mason Kelly (11)	186
Connor North (11)	187
Luke Seymour (11)	188
Annabel Baker (10)	189
James Sims (11)	190
Lloyd Jaques (11)	191

The Poems

Spirit

At the peak of the mountain he stands,
Holding his head high with pride.
As the Northern Lights appear behind him,
The magnificent colours light up his watchful eyes
With every colour imaginable.

Now it's his time to go,
He scans the land below him one last time,
Then a large pool of glitter floods the land.
The gates of Heaven have opened for him,
And the angels are waiting for him to return,
He is taken from the Earth.

Billie-Sioux Parsons (10)
Ardleigh St Mary's CE Primary School

Be Back By Nine Fifteen

'You can play in the park
Kick a ball till it's dark
As long as you're back by 9:15'

'You can go to France
And see your aunts
As long as you're back by 9:15'

'You can go to York
And get me some pork
As long as you're back by 9:15'

'You can play with a snake
Near a bottomless lake
As long as you're back by 9:15'

But what's going to happen at 9:15?'

Alexander Hawkins (9)
Ardleigh St Mary's CE Primary School

Buzzer

Slowly as the daytime creeps,
The buzzer loudly makes its speech,
Whizzing speedily from flower to flower,
Full of energy, bursting with power,
Anywhere light, sunny and bright,
Is what the buzzer considers right.

But when the sky is painted black,
The sun goes down, the moon comes back,
Very soon the buzzer stops gliding,
And instead it is secretly hiding.

Until the night-time fades,
Then it's amongst the verdant blades.

Lauren Smith (10)
Ardleigh St Mary's CE Primary School

If You Could Fly

If you could fly, with magic wings
You could do some wonderful things

If you could fly, fly to Spain
Fly to Spain, but not by plane

If you could fly, fly to Greece
Fly to Greece, to see the geese

If you could fly, fly to Dubai
Fly to Dubai, before you die

If you could fly, fly to Turkey
Fly to Turkey, to swim in the sea

If you could fly, fly to France
Fly to France, to do a little dance

Dance the night, dance the day
Dance in any simple way!

Madeleine Ray Peel (8)
Ardleigh St Mary's CE Primary School

Five Little Monkeys

Five little monkeys sitting on a bed,
Fred fell off and bumped his head,
Mummy called the doctor and he said,
'Still sit on the bumpy little bed.'

Four little monkeys sitting on a bed,
Charlie fell off and bumped his head,
Mummy called the doctor and he said,
'Still sit on the bumpy little bed.'

Three little monkeys sitting on a bed,
Ben fell off and bumped his head.
Mummy called the doctor and he said,
'Still sit on the bumpy little bed.'

Two little monkeys sitting on a bed,
Zoe fell off and bumped her head.
Mummy called the doctor and he said,
'Still sit on the bumpy little bed.'

One little monkey sitting on a bed,
She fell off and bumped her head.
Mummy called the doctor and he said,
'Put the monkey on the little bed.'

No little monkeys sitting on the bed,
None fell off and bumped their head.
Mummy called the doctor and he said,
'Get those monkeys to sit on the bed!'

Madeleine Peel (8)
Ardleigh St Mary's CE Primary School

The Leg-Eater

When in your bed
He hasn't been fed
So pull up your cover
And call for your mother
Now that your walls are red
You're *dead!*

Daniel Rogers (9)
Ardleigh St Mary's CE Primary School

Blossom

Candyfloss stuck on a tree
That's what blossom looks like to me
It's pink, it's white
It's sheer delight
It really is a glorious sight
Fluff on a tree
Lots of pink for you to see
When the wind blows
The petals explode
They flutter down in a whole big load
They look like fluff from under my bed.

Elizabeth Hawkins (8)
Ardleigh St Mary's CE Primary School

The Boy Of The Night

At the heart of the night,
Watch for the lone boy,
Waiting in the pale moon's light,
Eyes forever changing to ice . . .
To cloud . . .
To stars . . .
As it shines upon faded jeans,
Upon silver hair,
Polished leather glistens,
Half-wild,
Still slightly mad,
Bewildered by time,
Chained to the night,
He might hear a sound,
Shift into a moonbeam,
And be gone.

Sophie Chujor (11)
Ardleigh St Mary's CE Primary School

True Colours!

True Colours is really fun,
We do majorette competitions in the sun.
We shake our pompoms left to right,
Our orange and blue uniforms are all right.
We use batons as well,
Which we twirl,
And our hair is done by Michelle.
There is Katie who is really kind,
Tracy and Antje who are really fine.
We do complicated moves,
Which make sure we hardly ever lose.
In True Colours we have sweet tiny tots,
Radical juniors and funky seniors.
Majorettes is well cool,
You should try it, you will rule!

Rianna Delabruyere (11)
Ardleigh St Mary's CE Primary School

Castles Of Doom

The glistening castles of doom,
The innocent peasants with brooms,
With white horses out front,
And pencils so blunt,
The whole castle is a trap.

In the rusty castles of doom,
Where only pennies loom,
The peasants wear rags,
And large heavy bags,
But no one knows it's a trap.

In the ancient castles of doom,
No flowers or blossoms bloom,
With spaghetti each day,
No rise in their pay,
Now they know it is a trap.

Kathleen Parsons (11)
Ardleigh St Mary's CE Primary School

Birthdays

Birthdays are special, birthdays are great,
Especially a chocolate-flavoured birthday cake.
Colourful balloons and party games,
Don't forget the badges that show us your names!

Come on in and put down your presents
I'll certainly enjoy them, even the pheasants.
Let's play some games - your turn now,
Jump as high as you can,
As high as a cow!

Fizzy drinks, chocolate biscuits,
And the goody bags are full of lipsticks.
Now it's time to say goodbye
Remember the birthday cake, don't be shy!

Natalie Spicer (9)
Ardleigh St Mary's CE Primary School

Mare And Foal

Soft brown eyes gazing down
As the foal sleeps upon the ground,
His mother, starts to graze close by
The foal wakes up and catches her eye.

Up he gets, wobbly at first,
Trots over to Mum to quench his thirst.
She gently nudges him, so proud
As he swishes his fluffy tail.

After his drink he's ready to explore,
All four feet jump off the floor
With a buck and a kick, off he goes,
Always keeping on his toes.

Around the field he canters fast,
Whinnying to his mum as he goes past
Eventually though, slowing right down,
Trots back to Mum, to sleep on the ground.

Zoe Carey (8)
Ardleigh St Mary's CE Primary School

Giraffes

Giraffes live in the savannahs of Africa,
Giraffes so tall and graceful,
With bodies like a jigsaw puzzle,
Of cream and brown,
For camouflage in the savannahs of Africa.

Giraffes live in the savannahs of Africa,
Their tongues are very long and black,
As black as the night sky,
The sun is so hot, so when they feed,
Their tongue doesn't get sunburnt.

Giraffes live in the savannahs of Africa,
They are amazing animals bending their knees,
They drink the water from puddles and ponds,
Their neck curves like a bridge,
To drink the mineral water on the savannah.

Rhianna Sexton (10)
Goodmayes Primary School

Hate

Hate is black like a gooey black dragon
Hate sounds like a woman screaming
Hate tastes like slimy goo
Hate smells like smelly socks
Hate looks like an ugly witch
Hate feels like being frozen
Hate reminds me of when a fire happened.

Eoin Moylan (8)
Goodmayes Primary School

My Kitten Kenzo

My kitten, Kenzo, is as cute as a butterfly,
With his tail flicking all down the hall,
I don't give him food when his 'miaow' annoys me.

He waits for a cuddle after he eats,
He plays with squirrels,
He hates our neighbour, Rosie,
Because she is very noisy.

He comes with his sharp teeth in the morning,
To bite my finger, that's so irritating.

When we've played a lot,
I get very tired,
So then I go to sleep,
In my new bed shaped in a tyre.

Sharon Raja (11)
Goodmayes Primary School

My Big Sister

My big sister is very annoying,
Whenever she calls me it is very irritating,
When I don't listen to her she teases me,
Which is so upsettting.
'Nazihah, get me some crisps.'

I cry, cry the whole day worrying,
When will Mum come back home?
My big sister is as cheeky as a monkey,
She says every day,
'Nazihah, get me some water.'

She goes out every night,
Leaving me alone at home,
I have to do all the work,
'Nazihah, get me my books.'
Big sisters are so tiring.

Nazihah Jahan (11)
Goodmayes Primary School

Me To You

Today is not a birthday,
Today is not a party,
But today is a special occasion,
A message from me to you,
I don't know what to say,
But here I go.

A friend like you is what I need,
A friend like you is always there for me,
A friend as caring as you is like a person
Looking down on me,
A friend like you can be trusted.

And now I will always be there,
I will give you a hand,
I will give you a shoulder,
If you need someone to lean on,
You are like a little sister to take care of,
I will be a guardian angel as long as you need me,

Why do I send this message?
Guess, you will never know . . .

Natasha Kamhono (10)
Goodmayes Primary School

School

School is like a growing plant.
Each year you move up, your plant grows.
New friends you make, new leaves grow.
New soil laid down, a new playground made.

School is like a growing plant.
It is a place where you make new friends.
Your best friends are Spring Blossoms.
Enemies are deadly fungi.

School is like a growing plant.
But one day it has to die.
That day comes for secondary school.
Like a seed dispersed into the outer world.

School is like a growing plant.
When you have reached your new school.
Just a little watering and your seed grows once again.
But this plant doesn't know what it's in for.

Eleanor Riaye (11)
Goodmayes Primary School

Why Are Children So Disobedient?

Teachers are always asking
Why are children so disobedient?
Well I don't know,
But I have ideas.

Maybe they're always dreaming,
About flying pigs,
Or snow in July,
Children love dreaming.

They might be dreaming about . . .
World War III or aliens from Mars.
Maybe even robots owning the UK,
Or interactive whiteboards, but we've already got those.

They might not even be dreaming,
They might be just bored.
Or maybe even weirder,
They could be zombies.

Now I'm getting scared,
Of disobedient children.
Really, really scared,
God save me.

These are just ideas,
I don't really know,
Only disobedient children,
Know why they are disobedient.

Taher Hussain (10)
Goodmayes Primary School

Young

Young, too young to buy an MP3 player
Young, too young to play with a computer
Young, too young to go to a disco party
Young, too young to go to a primary school.

Young, too young to play a football match
Young, too young to play with a PlayStation
Young, too young to go in a casino
Young, too young to have a mobile phone.

Young, too young to have a TV
Young, too young to watch a movie of action
Young, too young to hear a scary sound
Young, too young to go to a bowling game.

Young, too young to help my mother clean the car
Young, too young to go to bed at midnight
Young, too young to drive a car
Young, too young to belong to a political party.

Why can't you do what you want?
Because you are just 3 years old
And you are too young!

Jean Pierre (11)
Goodmayes Primary School

Sisters, Sisters

Sisters, sisters,
So smart and pretty
They always help people
They are beautiful and kind.

Sisters, sisters,
Always put the TV on
Then they put the music up
They wake up early and moan.

Sisters, sisters,
Sisters are helpful
I love my sisters so much
And that is all about sisters.

Gurpreet Lall (8)
Goodmayes Primary School

Butterfly

Butterfly, butterfly
Fluttering in the wood
So alive in the air
And looking so good.

Butterfly, butterfly
Fluttering colours so bright
Your glorious wings
Could sparkle in the night.

Butterfly, butterfly,
Fluttering, where will you go?
Where is this place?
Has it got snow?

Leila Begga (9)
Goodmayes Primary School

April Fool's Day

I love April Fool's Day
There's lots of tricks that you can play.

Loads of tricks in every house
You could make a fake mouse.

Some people get in a mood
But they can eat lots of food.

So please come and do a trick or take the mick!

Jasmine Paul (9)
Goodmayes Primary School

Winter

Snow
Snow feels so frozen
The frost feels so cold
It's the time for snowboarding
The smell of hot chocolate and coffee
And lots of sleighs.
Snow
Snow
It's the time for kids to go out and play
Winter
Winter
Kids go to school.

Wayne Nwokolo (8)
Goodmayes Primary School

Summer

A nice summer
A golden and a shiny summer
Summer is best
Summer you can play anywhere
That's why I like summer
That's my summer.

Yadhav Yogeshwar Jayeprokash (9)
Goodmayes Primary School

Prince

Prince, prince
Riding on his horse
Galloping away to the princess
Of course!

Prince, prince
Rich but sometimes poor
Some are woodcutters and they break the law!

Prince, prince
Some of his stories are sad
It's a good thing he's not supporting
The bad!

Roubina Begum (9)
Goodmayes Primary School

Dolphins

Dolphins are cute
And they shimmer
And they're blue
And they might even
Kiss you!

The fish and the whales
Love the dolphins
Shining tail.

They are always happy to play
In the sea of course
With you and me!

Jenny Dixon (8)
Goodmayes Primary School

Rabbits

Rabbits, rabbits
Hopping everywhere
Twitching their noses
Here and there.

Rabbits, rabbits,
Jumping in and out of holes
Nibbling bits of grass
Bumping into moles.

Naomi November (9)
Goodmayes Primary School

Brothers

Brothers, brothers
So helpful and crazy
Drive people mad
They're so lazy.

Brothers, brothers
Who sleep too long
They work so tough
They sing so many songs.

Brothers, brothers,
Who are sometimes dumb
They gobble so much
They're so clever because they love sums.

Aarondeep Singh Johal (9)
Goodmayes Primary School

Alone

Lonely
Lonely

The tall, scary trees
In the dark empty street.

Scary
Scary
I hear a crash
As I walk down the road
I wish my friends could be here with me.

Wishing
Wishing.

Whitney Nwokolo (8)
Goodmayes Primary School

Spring - Haiku

Green leaves in the trees
Pink lotus flowers in grass
Like wet lily pads.

Santaj Nijjar (8)
Goodmayes Primary School

Football

Football, football
Is so much fun
Makes people mental
Just like the sun.

Football, football
Lots of people like the game
Most people think it's wild
Some think it's just lame.

Football, football
Score so many goals
People go crazy
And so do their souls.

Football, football
Some fans are furious
Most of them aren't
Far more are curious.

Ashraf Ahmed (9)
Goodmayes Primary School

Chocolate - Haiku

Scrumptious, luscious food
Delicious, delightful rolls
Like twirling spirals.

Shabnam Raji (9)
Goodmayes Primary School

Homework

Homework,
Homework,
One thing teachers make you do.
I hate it, what about you?
Homework's for budding teachers,
But not for human creatures,
Sometimes it's English,
But mostly maths,
Even some science,
It makes me feel a nuisance.
Homework, homework,
One thing teachers make you do,
I hate it, what about you?
I think it's such a bore,
I'd rather do my chores!
Do you like it?
I hate it! What about you?

Reshma Saleh (8)
Goodmayes Primary School

Uncle Frank

When we are asleep in bed,
My uncle Frank unscrews his head.
He fixes on another one,
And sets off for a night of fun.

It really gave me quite a jolt
The first time I saw the bolt
Which Uncle proudly showed to me
In the cellar after tea.

He really did give his fame
That is why we share a famous name.
Oh I forgot to tell you mine
Our family's name is Frankenstein!

Jef Vanstraelen (8)
Goodmayes Primary School

Summer

Summer sunshine is the brightest thing in my life.
The golden sun captures my eyes.
Summer strawberry, raspberries and bananas too.
The shiny sun is as bright as it can be.
People having fun in the sea.
The golden sun is shining brightly,
Children playing in the park.
Summer, vanilla, chocolate ice cream
And lemonade too.

Sushmithaa Amour (9)
Goodmayes Primary School

World Cup Fever 2006

Everyone is getting ready
It's almost here and maybe
We might win
In Berlin we will hold the cup
The golden cup
Everybody in England will line up
Just to see the bus
Then the whole world will know
The power of England.

Mohamed Zamdi (9)
Goodmayes Primary School

Spiders

Spiders are red
Spiders are green
Spiders are also very mean.

Spiders are long
Spiders are tickly
Spiders move very quickly.

Spiders are big
Spiders are scary
Spiders are also very hairy.

Hassan Sharif (9)
Goodmayes Primary School

Dragons

There lives a dragon
In a faraway land.
The big old dragon loves
To play with sand.
He isn't that old, he's only 36,
And hates any dirty tricks.
He eats a lot of honey
But it costs him so much money.
Stay away from him because
He's a little mad!
If you shout at him he'll become sad.
This is the dragon who lives in a faraway land.

Sukhneet Bhatia (9)
Goodmayes Primary School

Ronaldinho

As fast as a Ferrari,
As clever as a doctor,
As rich as a millionaire,
As tall as a giant,
As goofy as Bugs Bunny
Now that's Ronaldinho!

Shaheel Ahmed (9)
Goodmayes Primary School

Drogba

As clever as a genius.
As skinny as a stick.
As strong as a T-rex.
As fierce as an elephant.
As brave as a lion.
As violent as a wrestler.
As victorious as a cheetah.

Hasnain Butt (9)
Goodmayes Primary School

Cheetahs

A cheetah is fast
On the grass
They are spotty
But they don't go shopping!
A cheetah is a cheetah
And you are a meat-eater.
You can't see them because they run so fast
On the African grass.
They roar
And make claws
A cheetah can be camouflaged
On the yellow grass.

Akshay Bhandari (9)
Goodmayes Primary School

Thierry Henry

He was born to play football
Even from a young age
He has a big wage
Fast as a rocket
Footballers are the heroes
Clever as any professor
Skilful as the rest
One day he's the best
Plays all the matches
That's my hero, Henry.

Bertrand Dowuona (9)
Goodmayes Primary School

Grandad

Sucking his sweets
Looking for me
And having his tea.

Grandad, grandad
Watching films
Walking so slow
He loves me, that I know.

Grandad, grandad
So skinny
Breaking into pieces
Giving me chocolates.

Harsimrat Sehmi (9)
Goodmayes Primary School

Giants

Giants are big,
Giants are tall,
Have you ever seen a giant that is really small?
Some giants are good,
Some giants are bad,
Some giants are funny,
Some giants are mad!
Are they here?
Are they there?
Can they fit into a chair?
Giants are tall,
They're taller than trees!
Giants are big,
They're bigger than me!

Nicole Samuels (9)
Goodmayes Primary School

Dragons And Monsters

Dragons, big, red and scaly,
That's how most of them look.
But not the one I saw,
He was as fast as a cheetah.
With claws as sharp as razors
And as hard as diamonds.
I was walking alone when
Suddenly I heard a noise.
I looked behind me . . .
Nothing was there.
Wait! What was that?
Was it a giant gobbling spider?
Or an Anchiceratops?
Then it jumped out at me . . .
It was enormously gigantic
And wonderfully silver like moonlight.
Then it stopped and started talking.
It said in a deep, strong voice,
'Why is everyone afraid of me?
Why does everyone run whenever I come out?'
I just stood there, frozen . . .

Aisha Dowlut (9)
Goodmayes Primary School

The Lost Boy

Help, help!
I'm lost in the park
It is very scary
I wish Mary would come and help me
I'm lost under a tree
I'm screaming so someone can hear me

My mum was sad
And I was really mad
I wanted to see my family
So we could live happily
And live in my house again.

Tauheed Ali (8)
Goodmayes Primary School

Animals

Lions are fierce
Monkeys are loud
Pigs are fat
Horses are quiet.

Zebras are stripy
Elephants are huge
Cows are spotty
Giraffes are colourful.

Bears are dark
Rabbits are soft
Deer are brown
Chickens are clever.

Navpreet Bolina (9)
Goodmayes Primary School

Animals

That animal is great
But it doesn't have a mate.
Look at that snail
It's leaving a trail.
That nasty fat pig
Is wearing a wig.
The buzzy bee
Is looking at me.
My little brown dog
Is lost in the fog.
Look up at the sky
There's a little fly.
Up in the sky's a bat
Down below's a cat.
A van's holding a load
Underneath is a toad.
Dig a hole
You'll find a mole.
Animals are everywhere.
Do you like them here and there?

Aisha Dar (9)
Goodmayes Primary School

Thierry Henry

Thierry Henry
Always playing football
Doing kick-ups everywhere in Paris.
Trying to score goals with his head.
Always passing to his teammates,
Then scoring goals,
He lives in the streets of Paris.

Umair Ansari (9)
Goodmayes Primary School

Mum

My name is Mum
All I do is
Work and work
I do it morning till night
It's ever so boring.
I'm never angry but
I do go
Mad and
Mad.
I have two twins
One girl
One boy
They make me
Happy and
Happy
I will give my life for them
They always help me
Help and
Help.

Raihana Ali (9)
Goodmayes Primary School

My Wishes!

If I had five wishes
One of my wishes could be . . .

That the wind would blow gently against a cracked crystal window,
From an old deserted mansion.

If I had five wishes,
My second wish could be . . .
That never again, anyone would hear the
Howling of a lonely puppy crying in the rain.

If I had five wishes,
One of my wishes could be . . .
That I could always have the feeling of warm
Plain milk dripping on my tongue,
As it is my favourite drink.

If I had five wishes,
My fourth wish could be . . .
That I would always be able to feel the sensation of Kinder Bueno,
My favourite chocolate, melting on my finger,
And then licking my finger, and swallowing that creamy taste.

If I had five wishes,
One of my wishes could be . . .
That no longer people would look at each other,
With their eyes full of rage,
But yes, look at each other and greet each other, with tender love.

If I could wish as many wishes as I wanted,
These would be my first five wishes,
Because I think the world could be much better,
If it was all under *my* command.

Keyla Pacheco (10)
Goodmayes Primary School

The Magic Box

(Based on 'Magic Box' by Kit Wright)

I will put in my box . . .
The roar of an engine,
The soft tweet of a bird,
The giggles of children having fun.

I will put in my box . . .
The cold wind on my face,
Raindrops wetting my body,
Nose burning from the smell of smoke.

I will put in my box . . .
Flies whizzing past a Venus flytrap,
Leaping fish in a gurgling stream,
Stars shooting past the silent sky.

I will put in my box . . .
Sun in the palm of my hand
Eating it like a sweet cowboy on a broomstick,
And a witch on a horse.

My box is made from gold and steel all over,
My lid has a cross on it.

I will fly to Mars with my box
And eat all the chocolate you could ever imagine.
I will take my friends and ask them to come with their boxes,
Then have a picnic with my friends on Planet Pluto.

Halil Cetin-Kayali (10)
Goodmayes Primary School

My Magic Box

(Based on 'Magic Box' by Kit Wright)

In my magic box there is . . .
The sound of the sea crashing on the rocks,
The melodious singing of a robin,
The thunder crashing down like an earthquake.

In my magic box there is . . .
The feeling of excitement on my birthday,
Joy and happiness when you get a baby brother or sister,
The feeling of chocolate melting down your throat.

In my magic box there is . . .
The horizontal sunset on the Pacific Ocean,
Light of the sun on a tropical island,
Glorious colours of the rainbow.

In my magic box there is . . .
The hugs of Mum and Dad filled with love and care,
Laughter of my little sister while she is playing with me,
The fun I have with my grandma and grandad.

My magic box is made from . . .
Crystal all around,
With silver, gold gems decorating the box,
On the lid there is a bit of glitter.

I will fly with my box all around the world,
I will go on the moon with my box,
I will go inside my box to sit on the hundred-coloured rainbow.

Shaili Shah (10)
Goodmayes Primary School

God Gave Birth

God made a wonderful mother,
A mother who never grows old.
He made her smile of the sunshine,
And He moulded her heart of pure gold.
In her eyes He placed bright shining stars,
In her cheeks fair roses
You see God made a wonderful mother,
And He gave that dear mother to me.

Rajwant Veghal (9)
Goodmayes Primary School

Wonderful Mother

M is for the million times she has kissed me
O is for only she is not growing old
T is for treasure, the treasure lies beneath the heart
H is for heart, a heart from purest gold made from Malaysia's
   tallest mountain
E is for eye with that look of sweetness
R is for right and right she'll always be
   put it all together, it spells mother,
   a word that means the world to me!

Mandeep Kaur Bhopal (10)
Goodmayes Primary School

Anger

Anger is red like a devil,
Anger sounds like death,
Anger tastes like fire,
Anger looks like fighting,
Anger feels like boiling oil,
Anger reminds me of getting hurt.

Maymunah Ahmed (7)
Goodmayes Primary School

Friends Forever

Friends forever
Written with a pen
Sealed with a kiss
If you are my friend
Please answer this
Are you my friend or are you not?
You told me once but I forgot.
So tell me now and tell me true
So I can say I'm here for you.
If I die before you do,
I will go to Heaven and wait for you
So tell me if you are my friend
Then I can come and live again.

Sukhpreet Dhaliwal (8)
Goodmayes Primary School

Happiness

Happiness is red like love.
Happiness sounds like friendship.
Happiness tastes like a strawberry.
Happiness looks like a red rose.
Happiness feels like joy.
Happiness reminds me of my friends.

Laiqah Yousuf (8)
Goodmayes Primary School

The Foul Potion

Witches and wizards,
Snowstorms and blizzards,
Cook up a potion,
That will cause such commotion,
Elves will get stuck up shelves,
Fairies will grow hairy and beardy,
Fat cats,
Rotten rats,
Kids hiding under lids,
All because of the terrible stink!

Maryam Khan (9)
Goodmayes Primary School

The Maniacal Poem!

Four maniac brothers,
One went astray,
Three brothers left,
At least for today!

Three maniac brothers,
One was dead,
Two brothers left,
Ready for bed!

Two maniac brothers,
One flew away,
One brother left,
Ready for running away!

No maniac brothers,
No one to play with,
All the ghosts there,
Trying to stand it!

Soowaraj Chelvam (10)
Goodmayes Primary School

The Magic Box

(Based on 'Magic Box' by Kit Wright)

I will put in my box . . .
The fierce roar of the lion in the jungle,
The threatening, angry voice of the teacher telling me off,
The powerful sound of thunder in the sky.

I will put in my box . . .
The feeling of a smooth, gentle breeze,
The feeling of a warm hug from my mum,
The feeling I feel when people show me kindness.

I will put in my box . . .
Pretty flowers in a green garden,
Snow settling on the ground,
Trees swaying in the silent breeze.

I will put in my box . . .
My uncle's face when he sees me after three years,
My dad's face when he gets angry,
My two sisters celebrating.

I will put in my box . . .
Me skating on Planet Pluto,
Me riding on the ring of Saturn,
The sun in my room.

My box is made from
Pure gold,
Rock and hard ice,
Sparkly jewels.

I will fly in my box,
I will visit the heavens in my box,
I will be a star in my box.

Sunneth Lawrence (10)
Goodmayes Primary School

My Skeleton

My skeleton's white and bony,
But it's really moany.

I have a great big jolly skull,
Actually it's kinda dull.

Tall dangling neck,
Which is like a card deck.

After that a fat shoulder bone,
That's hanging all alone.

A long shaking spine,
For me that's just fine.

A bunch of dancing ribs,
Who all sleep in cribs.

Then a broad wide hip,
Sadly, it always likes to drip.

Next, my great fat, rattling thigh,
That gives a mean lie.

Have a jiggling knee,
Oh no, that's me.

Now my kicking leg,
But sometimes it looks like a hanging peg.

At last, the two big feet,
Which like to be neat.

Aamir Bilal Pirzada (10)
Goodmayes Primary School

My Magic Box

(Based on 'Magic Box' by Kit Wright)

In my magic box there is . . .

The sound of a massive baby crying,
The angel whispering while singing,
The soft tweet of a bird.

In my magic box there is . . .
The taste of a chocolate bird melting in my mouth,
My nose burning from the smell of smoke,
Cold ice cubes melting through my hand.

In my magic box there is . . .
A dolphin's fin shining like a bird,
Trees swaying in the wind,
The wave of a blue sea.

In my magic box there is . . .
Lemonade from a volcano,
The moon's light shining so bright,
A house made out of a sun.

My magic box is made of . . .
Logs, colours such as red, yellow, diamonds,
With shark's teeth around it.

I would go in a magic forest
Buy a magic carpet and fly on it
And I would go around the world in eighty days
To learn languages.

Shaniece Petrie (10)
Goodmayes Primary School

Hate

Hate is red like a boiling hot volcano.
It sounds like a breaking sound.
It tastes like people smoking.
It smells like smoke.
It looks like vomiting.
It feels like people dying.
Hate reminds me of a black cat
That came to me and tried to scare me.

Aadil Hafesji (7)
Goodmayes Primary School

Sadness

Blue like hay fever,
It sounds like tears coming down people's eyes,
It tastes like runny, smelly water.
It smells like rusty, smelly water.
It looks like rain dripping on the ground.
It feels like thorns pricking into my hands.
It reminds me of the wet, smelly water dripping on the rough ground
And people getting hurt.

Odilia Vanstraelen (7)
Goodmayes Primary School

Anger

Anger is red like a burning, flaming hot lava.
It sounds like lightning.
It tastes like molten lava.
It smells like petrol burning.
Anger looks like someone who is greedy.
Anger feels like salt in your mouth.
Anger reminds you of hatred.

Raja Hussain (8)
Goodmayes Primary School

My Dad

Fast like a cheetah
Short as a table
Lovely as the sea
Helpful like a friend
Nice as a teacher
That's my super dad.

Imran Javaid (8)
Goodmayes Primary School

Fear

Fear is black like a ghostly night.
It sounds like a dark, creepy night.
Fear tastes like a slimy slithering king snake.
It looks like an enormous hairy lion.
Fear feels like red blood.
It reminds me of bubbling red lava.

Nili Shah (8)
Goodmayes Primary School

Fear

Fear is red like blazing magma.
It sounds like lightning crushing on houses.
It tastes like rotten and melted cheese.
It smells like petrol spreading.
It looks like magma erupting.
It feels like red magma running down your body.
It reminds me of the fear people had before Kara Ktaa erupted.

Sameer Khan (8)
Goodmayes Primary School

Love

Love is red like a romantic rose
It sounds like people kissing
It tastes like sour ice cream
It smells like air-freshener
It looks like a rainbow
Love reminds me of love hearts
Floating in the air.

Shakira Simpson (8)
Goodmayes Primary School

Happiness

Happiness is like bright pink candyfloss.
Happiness sounds like children and adults laughing and laughing.
Happiness tastes like a bunch of lovely sweet pink icing cakes.
Happiness looks like lots and lots of people
Laughing and laughing and laughing together.
Happiness feels like a soft heart filled up with laughter.
Happiness reminds you of people and children having fun
With their friends, cousins, grandpa and grandma
And, of course, parents.

Tajinder Sanger (8)
Goodmayes Primary School

Sadness

Sadness is as blue as the crushing sea.
Sadness sounds like somebody crying.
Sadness is the taste of soft green Brussels sprouts.
Sadness looks like someone who is alone.
Sadness feels like no one is there.
Sadness reminds you of a rushing storm.

Obianuju Anyika (7)
Goodmayes Primary School

Anger

Anger is red like oozing blood.
It sounds like crashing cars.
It tastes like Brussels sprouts.
Anger feels like fire.
It reminds me of dead people.

Remika Sharma (7)
Goodmayes Primary School

Love

Love is red like roses.
It sounds like people having a big picnic.
It tastes like pink tasty candyfloss.
Love smells like beautiful romantic flowers.
Love looks like a red fluffy heart.
It feels like my mum's warm hands hugging me.
Love reminds me of my mum's wonderful wedding.

Hazvinei Kamhono (8)
Goodmayes Primary School

Noah Lot

Noah Lot is awfully smart
And loves to share his ideas.
He's only in second grade,
He ought to get lots of As.

His brain is like a dictionary
Which has a very good memory.
My teacher thinks he's wonderful
And treats him in a very good way.

The children on the other hand,
Think he's quite a bossy boy.
Being Noah Lot is quite out of hand
In my way.

He bores me with his rubbish lists
And very good trivia.
He ought to go to Insect Land
Right in Bolivia.

So that's my poem about Noah Lot.
It may be very embarrassing.
I wish I knew a bit like him
I just don't want to be that much dim.

Fatima Moosa (7)
Goodmayes Primary School

Happiness

Happiness is a colour of a blue peaceful life together.
It sounds like people waving their colourful kites.
It tastes like people enjoying their life.
It looks like people having and playing with their family.
It feels so calm and sweet.
It reminds me of happiness and love.

Nazira Tasnim (8)
Goodmayes Primary School

Love

Love is red like a giant rose.
Love sounds like a flower singing.
Love tastes like a lovely bit of honey.
Love smells like a lovely bunch of flowers.
Love looks like a big rainbow.
Love feels like someone is kind to you.
Love reminds me of people caring and helping each other with love.

Kyla Boyle (8)
Goodmayes Primary School

Sunny Days

Sunny days are as bright as stars
Sunny days are as blue as the sea
Sunny days are as sunny as Hawaii
Sunny days feel as warm as cuddles
Sunny day breezes taste as nice as coconuts
Sunny days reminds me of beaches.

Haleema Dar (8)
Goodmayes Primary School

Open The Door

(Inspired by 'The Door' by Miroslav Holub)

Open the door
What's outside?
Maybe a bear in fright
Or a giraffe with a light.

Open the door
What is outside?
Maybe a tiger
A bird flying in the sky up so high.

Open the door
What is really outside?
Maybe the sun, the sky
Or even a happy smile.

Jazmin Mitchell-Blake (8)
Goodmayes Primary School

Looking 4 God

You don't look for God,
God was never lost.
He died for our sins,
To pay the cost.
God is always with us wherever we go,
So don't be full of woe.
Where do I go when I'm feeling down?
Who do I call when friends aren't around?
I look to the lifter of my head,
Jesus my Saviour, Lord and friend.
The only way to find God is through prayer,
So don't act like you don't care.
'Cause you know that God is there,
He knows all the things we've been through,
He's always lovin' and true.
Our behaviour towards God is appalling,
Stop the chattin' and start applauding.
God will answer prayers.
Read your Bible, that's all you can do
Pray for me while I pray for you,
Nuff love
And God bless you 2.

Ellessi Ricketts (11)
Goodmayes Primary School

Hatred

Hate looks like lava's burning red.
Hate sounds like a dragon's roar.
Hate tastes like a spicy chilli burning taste.
Hate looks like a warrior's triumph.
Hate feels like a volcano erupting.
Hate reminds me of dragon stories.

Nadeem Mer (8)
Goodmayes Primary School

Hate

Hate is grey like the clouds.
It sounds like people having an argument.
It tastes like a rotten apple.
It smells like a stinky fart.
It looks like a cloud.
It feels like a rotten egg.
It reminds me of my mum and dad
Shouting at each other.

Amritral Singh Bhogal (8)
Goodmayes Primary School

Love

Love is a big red heart by a rose.
Love is like when red birds are singing in the sky.
Love tastes like a cold chocolate.
Love smells like fresh air in the sky.
Love looks like an enormous fab star.
Love feels like the two hands that join.
Love reminds me of my best friends and family
As everyone sees.

Filipe Santos (8)
Goodmayes Primary School

Friendship

Friendship is as green as grass.
Friendship sounds like birds cheeping.
Friendship tastes like chocolate.
Friendship smells like friends together.
Friendship looks like a group together.
Friendship feels like lots of colourful flowers in my hands.
Friendship reminds me of a group of friends together.

Samira Ahmed (7)
Goodmayes Primary School

Friendship

Friendship is green like grass.
Friendship sounds like somebody is playing with their friends.
Friendship tastes like chocolate.
Friendship smells like friends together.
Friendship looks like a group together.
Friendship feels like lots of flowers in my hand.
Friendship reminds me of a group of friends playing.

Ulfet Enver (8)
Goodmayes Primary School

Love

Love is red like a rose.
Love sounds like when you are with your family.
Love tastes like chocolate.
Love smells like perfume.
Love looks like a star in the sky.
Love feels like two hearts joined together.
Love reminds me of my grandma and grandad.

Sofia dos Santos (8)
Goodmayes Primary School

Friendship

Friendship as blue like the sky.
Friendship sounds like spray.
Friendship tastes like chicken and chips.
Friendship smells like ice cream.
Friendship looks like a teddy bear.
Friendship feels like water.
Friendship reminds me of my teacher.

Ameer Hamzah (7)
Goodmayes Primary School

Friendship

Friendship is as pink as lipgloss.
Friendship sounds like love.
Friendship tastes like chocolate cake.
Friendship smells like roses.
Friendship looks like friends.
Friendship feels like fresh air.
Friendship reminds me of my friends.

Sanah Mansoor (7)
Goodmayes Primary School

Anger

Anger is red.
Anger sounds like an angry person.
Anger tastes like hurting another.
Anger is like someone horrible is cooking.
Anger looks like someone getting cross.
Anger reminds you of someone getting hurt.

Simran Lotay (7)
Goodmayes Primary School

A Dog's Life

A dog's life is happy when she gets a home
A dog's life is happy when she gets a bone.

A dog's life is sad when she is told off
A dog's life is sad when she hears a cough.

A dog's life is when she is in pain,
A dog's life is when she is in the rain.

Elouise Atkins (10)
Hadleigh Junior School

A Ferrari's Life

This car is noisy and it is also very fast,
You should really buy it because this car is first class.
This thing is very shiny; the noise is loud and clear,
You should really see it when a rabbit is near,
It yipps and hits the accelerator pedal,
For a car that goes this fast you should give it a medal.
Finally it has to stop for the red light in the traffic,
You wouldn't like the noise that this car is unleashing.
When it crashes it smashes its light,
Oh, I'm blind, the one on my right!
With a petrol tank of over four litres in the car,
You should also go very, very far.

Daniel Allen (10)
Hadleigh Junior School

Imagination Of Life

High or low
Fat or thin
Dark or light
New or old
Dry or wet
Adult or child
A world can be big or small
It is the size of your imagination.

Cameron Heath (10)
Hadleigh Junior School

My Pet Cat

My pet cat was watching telly
In ran the hamster and jumped on his belly
Boing, bounce, bounce, boing
The cat was thinking, *how annoying*
The hamster bounced up onto the light
Boy it gave that creature a fright
It went and clattered back down to earth
Flat! Splat!
It got devoured by the cat.

Liam Conley (9)
Hadleigh Junior School

Doctor Who Time Adventures

A whirling whooshed around the Powell Estate,
Fixed was Rose Tyler's fate.
A massive blue box suddenly arrived,
A man appeared from inside.
Rose asked, 'Have you committed a crime?'
The strange man answered, 'No, I travel through time.'
'How do you do that? Or is it just grime?'
They travelled back to a big kerfuffle,
It was a place without a truffle.
Next they met cat nuns,
But they had claws not guns.
Then they met Queen Victoria,
And a werewolf called Gloria.
A whirling whooshed around the Powell Estate,
Finally Rose could
See her mate!

Alec Waymark (10)
Hadleigh Junior School

My Cat Called Cindy

I have two cats and one big dog,
One cat ran away because of a log!
Now all that's left is one cat and a cool big dog!
When she came along, I mean Tulip,
We had to get rid of the dog.
Now all that's left is my cat, Cindy,
So furry and yet so windy!
My cat called Cindy purrs around me,
Does yours? My cat does.
Yellow eyes.
Chicken pies,
Attracts all the guys!

I now have one cat called Cindy.

Montana Clarke (10)
Hadleigh Junior School

Football

Football, wonderful football
Travels in the sky
Never going to die
Football, do you like football?
Football, wonderful football?
Travels at the speed of light
Moves with the wind
Football, do you like football?
Because I do.

Steven Potter (10)
Hadleigh Junior School

Giraffe

Giraffe was born

For its long neck,
It took the thickness of a trunk of a tree.
It took the thinness of a branch.
It took the coldness of the leaves.

For its slithery tongue,
It took the smoothness of the piece of paper.
It took the strength of a rubber.
It took the length of a ruler.

For its patchy fur coat,
It took the gold of the sun.
It took the brownness of a chocolate bar.
It took the splodges of a car.

For its round horns,
It took the roundness of a rainbow.
It took the bumpiness of a camel's back.
It took the softness of a pillow.

Giraffe was made.

Ellie-Jade Smith (11)
Hadleigh Junior School

Kangaroo Began

Kangaroo began,
She took the spring of the slinky,
She took the strength of the wind,
And made the power of her legs.

For her eyes,
She took the blackness of the berries,
She took the shine of the sun,
She took the brightness of the stars.

For her tail,
She took the crop from a horse,
She took the swish of the trees,
She took the slice of a sword.

For her home,
She took the heat from the candle,
She took the prickles of the holly bush,
She took the yellow from the sand.

For her voice,
She took the whisper from the sea,
She took the high pitch of the wind,
She took the flow of the river.

Kangaroo was made.

Anna Goldup (10)
Hadleigh Junior School

Dolphin Dived

Dolphin dived,
She took the glistening of the sun,
She took the smoothness of leather,
For her skin.

Dolphin dived,
She took ground peppercorns,
She took the shine of the moon,
For her beautiful eyes.

Dolphin dived,
She took the quickness of the wind,
She swept the leaves from the trees,
For her fast flippers.

Dolphin dived,
She took the loving of a heart,
She took the coldness of the ice,
For her salty blue lips.

Dolphin dived,
And was made.

Ella Glazier (10)
Hadleigh Junior School

Curtains

(Inspired by 'The Door' by Miroslav Holub)

Go and open the curtains,
Maybe there's a bee outside,
Or a flower,
Or a person.

Go and open the curtains,
Maybe there's a bottle of milk,
Or a fly,
Or some beautiful clouds.

Go and open the curtains,
Maybe there's the newspaper,
Or a box,
Or a letter.

Jodie Purser (7)
Hadleigh Junior School

The Laptop

(Inspired by 'The Door' by Miroslav Holub)

Go and open the laptop,
Maybe there's an unwanted document
Or an error
Or a secret site.

Go and open the laptop,
Maybe Smart Notebooks
Or Microsoft Word
Or Internet Explorer.

Go and open the laptop,
Maybe there's a wondrous screensaver
Or an alien
Or just fresh air.

Ben Aldridge (8)
Hadleigh Junior School

The Loft

(Inspired by 'The Door' by Miroslav Holub)

Go and look in the loft
Maybe you'll find an old toy!
Or an old T-shirt
Or a ripped blanket.

Go and look in the loft
Maybe there is a genie
Or an ancient poster
Or an old scrapbook!

Lucy Berry (8)
Hadleigh Junior School

The Attic

(Inspired by 'The Door' by Miroslav Holub)

Go and open the attic
Maybe there's a case,
Or an abandoned photo book,
A puppet
Or a stargazer.

Go and open the attic
Maybe there's an army jacket,
Or a golden chair,
An old message,
Or a secret passage
To an enchanted lair.
Go and open the attic.

Sophie Poyser (9)
Hadleigh Junior School

Go And Look In The Chest

(Inspired by 'The Door' by Miroslav Holub)

Go and look in the chest
Maybe there's diamonds or coins
Maybe a gold necklace.

Go and look in the chest
Maybe it covers a secret passage
Or an underground land
Maybe a magic castle.

Go and open the chest
Maybe it leads to a giant chess board.
Who knows, just go and open it.

Niall Manning (8)
Hadleigh Junior School

The Mysterious File

(Inspired by 'The Door' by Miroslav Holub)

Go and open that file
Maybe there's a letter of luck,
Or maybe there's something vile,
Or maybe there's a bill,
Two times heavier than me.

Go and open that file
Maybe there's paper as white as snow
Let's hope it's not dark and gloomy
Or maybe you have to fill in a form
(So boring!)

Go and open that file
Try to get your head around it
You will have to do it sooner or later!

Samuel Charman & Charlotte Crudgington (8)
Hadleigh Junior School

Go And Open The Pencil Case

(Inspired by 'The Door' by Miroslav Holub)

Go and open the pencil case,
Maybe there's a golden pencil
Inside waiting to be used.
Or a rubber,
Or a sharpener,
Or colouring pencils.

Go and open the pencil case,
Maybe there's pens waiting to be used,
Or a ruler,
Or a left-over pen with no ink left,
Or Tipp-ex,
Or gel pens.

Go and open the pencil case,
Maybe there's some paint inside,
Or a paintbrush,
Or a marker pen,
Or there's nothing inside.

Frankie Bird (8)
Hadleigh Junior School

The Box

(Inspired by 'The Door' by Miroslav Holub)

Go and open that box
Maybe there's a hidden treasure
Waiting to be found,
All gold and shiny.

Go and open the box
Maybe there's a beautiful castle
Or a hidden land
Or a dirty scummy underground.

Go and open that box
Maybe there's a giant chessboard
Waiting to be played.

Go and open the box
Maybe there's a chocolate factory
Waiting to be opened.

Who knows?
It might just be your imagination.

Rhys Watson (9)
Hadleigh Junior School

My Purple Checkered Bicycle

It's summertime again and I'm ready to go
Zooming up and down, falling in the summer glow.
Seeing all the butterflies flow
And doing the loop-the-loop.
My owner comes and rides me again
Turning my pedals, watching leaves blow,
Saying hi to neighbours in that summer glow,
'But not that anymore,' says the other bicycle on the ground floor.
'You will never get to the open door.
You will have to stay on the ground floor.'
I wish I was riding in the wind,
But not now, not ever, for I am just a checkered bicycle.

Leigh-Marie Hobday (10)
Hadleigh Junior School

My Friend, Isabella

F riendly faces looking at me
R ude is the thing which she is not
I sabella plays with me
E njoying the time I spend with her
N ever being rude or impolite
D ainty feet whenever she's dancing.

Tara Pomery (8)
Hamilton Primary School

My Maisy

My dog is called Maisy
We love going for walks together.
She loves getting dirty
She is spotty and dotty
Excited and potty
She is very playful
And loves to chew my slippers
At night she sleeps at the end of my bed.

Sian King (8)
Hamilton Primary School

A Cat Called Piggy

She is silky brown
And I love to stroke her
She likes to sit on the stairs
And watch with her lovely blue eyes
There is a dog next door
When she runs into the house
All you can see is her brown furry tail.

Lily Morgan (7)
Hamilton Primary School

Parents

P arents are always in the way
A nd they always do silly dances
R eally silly ones. They
E mbarrassed me at my party
N ever do that again, Mum and Dad, OK?
T rying to be cool -
S ometimes they are.

Melissa Armstrong (8)
Hamilton Primary School

The Weather

This morning it is spring,
And all the plants grow fast,
People like the spring so much,
They're glad it isn't last.

The day of spring has changed,
It has become so hot,
Some of the flowers died of the heat,
And some of the flowers did not.

Now the weather has changed a lot,
It happens to be autumn,
Now the leaves fall off the trees,
So you have to say you caught them.

The weather is now winter,
It is now freezing cold,
Then the weather goes back to spring,
And that's what I've been told.

Alex Galloni (10)
Hare Street Junior School

Accident Prone

My name is Chelsey,
I've broken a bone,
I've had bumps and bruises,
I'm accident prone.

I go to the hospital
With sickness and pain,
I've been so many times,
It drives me insane.

I've been on crutches
And I've had a bandaged arm,
Injections and blood tests,
But I've come to no harm.

I've had X-rays and wheelchairs,
And my head in a brace,
To prevent more injuries,
Just in case.

The doctors and nurses
Are kind and polite,
They tend to my injuries,
Whether morning or night.

Though I don't like hospitals,
It's not bad at all,
Because on the bright side,
I don't have to go to school.

Chelsey Compton (10)
Hare Street Junior School

I Can Beat Beckham

I can beat Beckham,
Captain of England,
No problem,
When he makes a big mistake
He sends Real Madrid bottom.

He played for United,
A few seasons ago,
He wanted to play longer,
But Ferguson said, 'No!'

I'm sure I'm faster than Beckham himself,
Couple more seasons,
He'll be on the shelf.

I can beat Beckham,
I know I can,
Other than that,
I'm his number one fan.

Conor Harrison-Luby (10)
Hare Street Junior School

Surfing

Surfing through the water
Slicing all the waves
Skirting along the surface
In the lifeguard's gaze.

Chopping up the water
Seizing all the fish
The sun is going down
In the water's mist.

Surfing across the rocks
Everyone's on the dock
You're full of dare
Can you dare, beware.

Just across the Channel
A shark is on its way
Quick, ready to get away?

Ross Squires (10)
Hare Street Junior School

My Dad

Dad works all day and night,
He never comes in sight.
I wish I was just like him,
Rather than that I am quite slim.

Dad's a hard worker,
He's definitely not a shirker,
He is very cool,
He could even fight a duel.

He is very brave,
And does like to shave,
He's not very monotonous,
I think that's quite obvious.

He is a strong man,
Even without his nan,
He cares for others,
Especially his brothers.

Saleem Mohammad (10)
Hare Street Junior School

Shopping In New York

When I get my money
I don't waste it on a lot
I get my bag on the sofa
And rush over to the shop.

I get on the plane
I talk to the hostess
Because everyone knows
That I am the best.

I go in the shops
Look around for a bit
I see all the tops
That are brightly lit.

Now it's time to go
I hope I'm not forgotten
Because I've got the
Best hair and that's made out of cotton.

I get back home
I really enjoyed it
Yes, I want to go back
I want it every bit.

Marjorie Sunday (10)
Hare Street Junior School

Best Of Football And The Worst!

Best of football is scoring great goals
And doing the best cheer!
Best of football is doing good passes
And reaching from person to person!
Best of football is winning a game
And winning a cup!

Worst of football is losing a game
And losing a cup final!
Worst of football is missing an open goal!
Worst of football is being in goal
And letting goals in!

And the really worst is getting hurt
Like breaking your leg.

But football is the best.

Bradley Perry (10)
Hare Street Junior School

The Wrestling Poem

I want to be a wrestler
I want to be on stage
I want to fight Ric Flair
But only if I dare.

I need to build my muscles
So I'll start eating Brussels
Weights in the gym
Will help me limb by limb.

The Boogeyman wants to take my heart
I won't let him win
I'll pin him down
And spin him round
And toss him in the bin.

I once saw John Cena
He looked really tough
He also looked buff
If I face him it will be rough.

Jack Campbell (10)
Hare Street Junior School

Great Girl

I'm a great girl
The most powerful girl in town,
I'm outstanding and furious,
But I don't know how.

I'm into fashion,
Not into bling,
Jeans and Converses
Are definitely my thing.

I like to dance,
Put my arms out and spin,
In every competition,
I'm gonna win.

I was born with talent,
I was born with fame,
I was born to be the best,
But people say I'm insane.

I'm a great girl
The greatest girl in town.
I'm outstanding and furious,
But I don't know how.

Alice Cracknell (10)
Hare Street Junior School

There's A Googly Monster

There's a googly monster
Lurking in the streets
Looking like an ordinary person
Eating lots of sweets.

If you see him
Run with all your might
Kick him, punch him
You've all got the right.

If he slows down
And you're huffing and puffing
Run home as fast as you can
And eat Mum's muffin.

You think it's all over
There's something in your bedroom
You're hiding under your covers
Or I should assume.

You wake up the next day
To get some yummy toast
You go to his favourite place
That he likes the most.

You're walking along the stream
In the monster's wide-open gaze
There's something coming up
And it looks like a maze.

The monster goes in
You go around
You hear something
Behind the big mud mound.

The monster comes out
He runs into the stream
He's gone for good
And you leave with a scream.

Danielle Fry (10)
Hare Street Junior School

Shopping

When you get money, go to the shops
Because you can guarantee you'll get cute tops
You can get skirts and lots of shoes
But when you buy them there'll be lots of queues.

People love the shops, how can you not?
Because when you buy something you look really hot
Go to the top floors, they're the best
Because I always look better than the rest.

So don't waste your time sitting on the sofa
Read a magazine or maybe a brochure.

Louise Orme (10)
Hare Street Junior School

Who Is Really My Best Friend?

Oh Chelsey is my best friend, my best friend
Oh Chelsey is my best, the best that there can be.
Until she broke my new pen, my new pen, my new pen,
Until she broke my new pen
Now we're not friends
You see!

Now Sophie is my best friend,
My best friend, my best friend,
Now Sophie is my best friend,
The best that there can be.
Until she beat my test mark,
My test mark, my test mark,
Until she beat my test mark
She can't be better than me!

So Alex is my best friend,
My best friend, my best friend,
I like her better you see
Until she spoke to Sophie
To Sophie, to Sophie,
Until she spoke to Sophie
She can't do that to me!

But now I have no best friend,
No best friend, no best friend,
But now I have no best friend I'm lonely as can be.
I think I want to make up,
To make up, to make up,
I think I want to make up,
Be friendly with all three!

But will they all forgive me?
Forgive me, forgive me?
But will they all forgive me
I've changed
They'll have to see!

Chusdey Bravo (10)
Hare Street Junior School

Queen Victoria

Sad looking Queen
In a grotto of glass
Sitting to be admired
By the people that pass.

Trina Brown (8)
Hare Street Junior School

The Eagle

Staring with evil eyes
Looking right at you
Perched on columns
Cruel looks
Fierce curved beak
Outspread wings
Ready to swoop
And grab you.

Megan Preston (7)
Hare Street Junior School

The Eagles

Twin eagles standing,
Up very high,
Watching with eerie eyes,
Getting ready to fly,
Guarding the gateway,
To the garden.

Jack Parker (8)
Hare Street Junior School

I Love Summer

Summer, summer, lovely outside
Everyone loves summer
Trees are bent like they're dancing
Little plants growing fine.

It's summer, the leaves are shining
The colour is bright green
The leaves are all happy and healthy
They are all shining like angels.

Happiness is always in summer
Without sun, no smiles
Everyone loves summer.

Tatenda Mapanda (10)
Hare Street Junior School

This Christmas Year

It's the start of Christmas and we're getting ready,
We put the holly on the gate in the fresh, cool winter air,
Where the snow is glistening all around.
All you can see of last season's grass
Is little blades poking out of the soft white snow.
The lantern is burning outside above the holly
At the front of the house.

The snowmen that we built earlier today
Are still standing happy and proud.

Chantal Collier (11)
Hare Street Junior School

Here Comes Spring!

Today is the first day of spring,
Freshly cut grass I can smell.
Green and yellow trees I can see.
A wonderful breeze filled with lovely smells.
Snow on mountains, turning into springs.
At last, at last spring is here!

The river is silently rushing, singing a song,
Blue skies filled with white clouds.
Birds singing, praising that it's spring.
Animals peeking through the trees.
Spring is here, don't let it go.

Somewhere, faraway children are saying bye to winter,
Children saying hello to playing out.
Some other children sad to say goodbye to their snowman.

I am happy spring is here,
Nothing can take its place.
Winter will come again, but for now let's rejoice!

Lindiwe Sikabe (10)
Hare Street Junior School

Spring!

Springtime has begun,
Now it's time to have some fun.
Planting bulbs and your seeds,
Now it's time to dig up weeds!

Splashing around in the pool,
It is really fun and cool,
There is a really cool breeze,
And the bees are buzzing in the trees!

Natalie Smyth (11)
Hare Street Junior School

Why I Like Christmas

I like Christmas because of the big footprints
On the snowy white ground.
The crunchy sound of the snow, the joy of making frost and the
Fresh smell of the falling snow.

The loud snap of the tree trunk,
The funny-shaped trees with the dark brown cliff leaning over me.

The blinding sun with the chilly shade
The bright winter sky with soft, calm sounds.

Ashley Clark (11)
Hare Street Junior School

The Metal Bird

Metal bird
About to fly
Up to the sky
Beak pointing up
Wings spreading out
Feet stuck to the ground
He cries,
'Please wait for me!
I do want to fly.'

Jahid Abdul & Sophie-Leigh Dangerfield (8)
Hare Street Junior School

The Owl

Standing stiff and silent
Gazing at the garden,
Watching people pass by,
See their own reflections,
In its empty eyes.
Shiny mirror body watching
The sun float by with the clouds and sky.

Macie Harwood-Turner & Jone McKeever (8)
Hare Street Junior School

Breezy

Quiet sunny day with nice chilly breeze.
Smooth green grass with juicy berries.
Long hard wooden branches with colourful leaves.
Red berries growing on bushes.
Lovely warm sun giving me a tan.
Fresh air keeping me healthy.
Beautiful smell of cut grass.

Mason King (10)
Hare Street Junior School

Precious Memories

An old lady
Somewhere on the beach, sits an old lady
Hearing children's laughter in her head.

An old lady
Somewhere on the beach sits an old lady
Remembering the fun she once had.

An old lady
Somewhere on the beach sits an old lady
Longing to see her childhood friends.

An old lady
Somewhere on the beach sits an old lady
Remembering what is left of precious memories.

An old lady
Somewhere on the beach sits an old lady
Wishing she had never grown old.

Elen McKeever (10)
Hare Street Junior School

Winter's Like A Show!

The cliffs are like big wooden stages,
The clear blue sky is like the ceiling of a theatre,
The sun shines like spotlights!

A fresh smell spreads through the air,
There's silence in the distant crowd.
The glittering snow is like glitter thrown to the floor!

The different shaped trees make shadowy patches, like people in
the dark.

Funny-shaped footprints to solve a mystery,
The wind whistles like the crowd cheering!

But the worst part of all, is when spring comes
And the show ends!

Aileen O'Reilly (11)
Hare Street Junior School

The Joy Of Winter

A little leaf, its house covered in snow.
A snowman sitting there, thoughtless.
A fireplace, burning up our souls.
The frozen lake, drowning our sorrows.

The empty park, reminding us of rainy days.
The snowball hitting the frozen face of gloom.
The smell of your favourite meal making you ill.
The laughter of children at Christmas, sounding like
                                    helpless screams.

That's the joy of winter!

Jaidene Neal (11)
Hare Street Junior School

Sunny Day

Hot sunny day so soft but not grey,
Green grass with shadows all day.
Red berries, brown leaves falling to the ground,
So dry but calm, light as day.
Blue skies light, bright and warm,
Leaves flying through the air,
What a beautiful day, with all there is to say.

Jake Budd (11)
Hare Street Junior School

Deep Ocean Mountain

Deep ocean mountain flying high.
Growing caves and warm sunny beaches picking spiky petals along
the mud
And then some hikers soaking up the view along the cliff
Watching eggs hatching near some flowers.
Then I see a gullible flower growing high, going to hit the warm
summer sky.
Special green leaves falling into the deep blue ocean
And then feeling the breeze on my face making my birthday a warm,
happy summer day.

Rough, heavy rocks squashing the roots and soil underneath the
deep ocean mountain
No one travelling up the rock to see the bees and the sad clouds that
hover above,
Sitting on the sky watching everyone doing activities
Swimming in the deserted ocean watching the animals underwater
live and die.
What a time at the deep ocean mountain.

Sunshine shining through the sand scaring the clouds and making
them rain.

The waves start to move and I start to run
Never again will I see deep ocean mountain.

Reece Nelson (10)
Hare Street Junior School

My Dream For Riding

I want to ride a horse out
On an open field where the sun
Is gleaming all night and day.

The horse of my dreams will come
Galloping towards me,
'Can I have my special horse tea?'
It would say to me.
Neigh, neigh, neigh, neigh.

If I get on it,
I will canter all around
But if it walks backwards,
It might lay on the ground.
So I will have to kick it on,
Then it will trot,
Well I have to go,
'Cause I have told you the whole lot.

Sophie Vanderhoven (10)
Hare Street Junior School

Deep Up In The Sky

Up in the sky the sunrays and birds fly by,
An eagle stares at its prey with its sharp eyes
Looking like a devil,
The sharp twigs looking fresh
And the trees leaves looking bright as can be.

Bilal-Ben Sghaier (11)
Hare Street Junior School

Rocky Mountains

Fresh snow on rocky mountains.
Rushing river below the steep hills.
Bright green grass sparkling in the bright orange sun.
Where dark mud lays beneath the hills.
Rushing river alive, breezy air passing by,
The bright blue sky shining.

Danny Lowles (11)
Hare Street Junior School

The Magic View

As I look into the magic view
I can smell all the different smells
The aroma-filled breeze and animal life in the forest.

Your nickname could be green scene,
Since you're covered in green.
Your river is so clear,
Just like a summer sky.

I can hear wood being chopped in the distance,
With tall trees swaying in the breeze.
Rushing water going downstream,
Away and away on an everlasting cycle.

Colourful flowers rustling,
Dazzling all who see,
This is my ode to the magic view
Which certainly dazzled me.

Jordan Gregg (10)
Hare Street Junior School

A Winter's Death

Walking down the bank covered with snow
Nobody was there, I was all alone.
I saw my reflection in the river
I was so cold I began to shiver.

The cold wind passed by my frozen face,
My footprints were left in the snow.
I wanted to walk home, I couldn't find my way.

I went and sat on the freezing ice,
My soul began to freeze.

Shannon Lockhart (10)
Hare Street Junior School

The Magnificent Rat

My rat is cute and cuddly like a cloud
His feet are small and pink
Like a small pebble and as soft as sand.
His fur is black and white.
His fur is soft and smooth.
His cage is big and silver like a dungeon.
He resembles spicy mouse.
I will feed and water him every day.

Reece Poulter (9)
Hare Street Junior School

The Magnificent Pony

My pony is white with grey spots
Like a grey rain cloud falling from the sky.
His feet are like a shoe clicking across the field,
His tail is like a fluffy chihuahua.
His eyes are like the blue sky.
He resembles the white and grey rain cloud.
I will really look after my pony forever and ever.

Charlie Burford (8)
Hare Street Junior School

My Magnificent Elephant

My elephant is gigantic like a mountain,
His trunk is like a fountain,
His feet are like rocks,
His ears are like flaps like a flag,
He resembles a big blue sky,
I will protect and feed forever.

Sharan Chandran (8)
Hare Street Junior School

The Magnificent Tiger

My tiger is massive like a tree
His whiskers are like sharp needles
His paws are like sharp pencils
His legs are like tree branches
He resembles a lion
I will love my tiger.

Samina Abdul (9)
Hare Street Junior School

The Magnificent Kitten

My kitten is small
Like a leaf on a tree
His tail is like a hosepipe
His forehead is as smooth as a person's face
His eyes are like blue marbles
He resembles a small mouse
I will protect my kitten.

Jayde Perry (8)
Hare Street Junior School

The Future - Haiku

What's in the future?
Flying cars and motorbikes
Hover beds and chairs.

Travis Prudence (9)
Hare Street Junior School

All Four Winds

The spring wind is
Fresh and gentle as
It blows through your hair
Like your head being tickled.

The summer wind is
Caressing and sweet as
It brushes the grass
Like the ripples on the sea.

The autumn wind is
Strong and naughty as
It picks the rubbish up
And hurls it down
Like houses being smashed
Up by a hurricane.

The winter wind is
Evil and grumpy as
It bangs on your window
Like a robber trying to
Break in.

Aylis Emek (8)
Hare Street Junior School

The Sizzling Wiggerling Sun

The sizzling wiggerling sun makes you want to have fun.
Laughter fills the air, no one really cares.

Seagulls sweep and dive
And the snap of a fish tells you it's alive
The ice cream man tells you it's ice cream time once again.

The smell of burgers, sniffing up people's noses,
Lay and whiff the open world.

Charlotte Taylor (9)
Manford Primary School

Homer Simpson

Homer Simpson is a fat and lazy man,
And he would eat anything out of a frying pan.
He never helps around the house, and when he's eating a doughnut
He is as quiet as a mouse.
When he is watching TV and drinking Duff beer,
He just drinks and drinks and sleeps and snores,
And that is the loudest thing you can hear.
He strangles Bart,
And does really smelly farts,
That you can smell from miles away.
So if you ever meet him, you'd better run
Because it will not be a pleasant day.

Harry Savage (9)
Manford Primary School

That's The Beach In Portugal

The crystal deep blue sea,
Shines from the crystal clear sky,
You can see the rugged cliffs,
That's the beach in Portugal.

You can feel the smooth sea,
Sparkling on the soft sand.
The air is very warm,
That's the beach in Portugal.

You can hear the seagulls squawking,
You can hear the swish of the sea,
The sand crunches under your feet,
That's the beach in Portugal.

You can smell the salty sea,
You can smell the juicy juice,
You can smell the sweet flowers,
That's the beach in Portugal.

You can taste the rough sand,
You can taste the drink and food,
You can taste the salty sea,
That's the beach in Portugal.

Shani-Maia Anderson (9)
Manford Primary School

It's Like This In Portugal

I see the rocks rolling,
I see the seagulls flying,
I see the shiny salty sea,
It's like this in Portugal.

I taste the shiny salty sea,
I taste the seaweed swim,
I taste the food in my mouth,
It's like this in Portugal.

I hear the seagulls squawking,
I hear the wind wafting,
I hear the waves whooshing,
It's like this in Portugal.

I smell the salty sea,
I smell the wind wafting,
I smell the suncream,
It's like this in Portugal.

I feel the streaming sunbeam,
I feel the sand crunching,
I feel the water whooshing,
It's like this in Portugal.

Hami Hossain (9)
Manford Primary School

Untitled

A butterfly swooping in the sky, fluttering.
I'm a butterfly when I come out of my cocoon the next day.
I'm a butterfly every day I swoop in the sky, I'm a butterfly.
Then next it's summer, why I like to bother.
I'm a butterfly, flying is my thing.
I'm a butterfly but the one thing I would like to say,
Am I bothered?

Safia Ewers (9)
Manford Primary School

Portugal

Birds tweeting loudly upon a branch.
Waves washing the sandcastle away.
Children splashing on the beach having fun,
Talking to each other, going to the beach.

Vanilla ice cream smelling as nice as a flower.
Salted water up my nose, smelling disgusting.
Coca-Cola smells like a rose in a garden.
Fresh air, smelling fresh as can be.

Sandy water in my mouth tasting like carrots,
Salt in my mouth tasting as disgusting as can be.
Ice cream in my mouth, tasting like I've never tasted before,
My drink is making my mouth refreshing.

See the birds flapping their wings just like a penguin.
Water's waves slashing upon the rocks.
The rocks are getting drenched by the water.
The sky is bright blue like a swimming pool's water.

Water splashing upon my body making me hot.
Feeling the shells on my feet making me shout, *ouch!*
The sand on my feet crunching and crunching under my feet,
Feeling the bucket upside-down filled with sand.

Alfie Smith (9)
Manford Primary School

Like Portugal

The squeaking seagulls I can see are pure white like silk.
I hear waves swooshing and swaying and roaring like lions.
I feel heat of the sun burning my skin.

I feel water of the sea as I swim.
I jump under the water, then salt water gets in my mouth.
I smell suncream as I walk past people.

I taste sand as I fall over,
I taste lollies and ice cream.
I hear lots of people talking,
I smell the sea and salt.

I see people sunbathing,
I fill the breeze of the wind.
I taste clean water everywhere,
I see ice cream.

I smell interesting smells.
I see Portuguese people.
I smell sand from the beach.
I see mountains everywhere.

Gabriella Long (9)
Manford Primary School

Portugal

You can see seagulls squawking above,
Children making sandcastles,
The water crashes against rocks,
The sun shines lots in Portugal.

You can hear the shell crabs scuttling round,
The crunching of the sand under your feet,
The people talking as they sunbathe,
The sun shines lots in Portugal.

It feels wet as the tide comes up,
The sea feels warm as you swim in it,
There's lots of different sizes of shells,
The sun shines lots in Portugal.

The food tastes very delicious,
And the drinks really refresh you,
When you're playing you get sand in your mouth,
The sun shines lots in Portugal.

The flowers smell quite different
And the salty water tastes bad.
You can smell the fruity suncream,
The sun shines lots in Portugal.

Jessie Allen (9)
Manford Primary School

In Portugal

I can see the sea shining and the flowers colourful as a rainbow,
And the rocks as hard as a metal,
It is like this in Portugal.

I can hear the beautiful seagulls making clucking noises,
And I can hear the waves going whoosh,
It is like this in Portugal.

I can feel the sand crunching on my hand,
And I can taste the fresh water and the shiny salty water,
It is like this in Portugal.

I can smell the yummy smell of the suncream,
And the fresh flowers and the fresh food,
It is like this in Portugal.

The fresh nice smell of the fruits,
And the food smell so nice,
It is like this in Portugal.

Odean Johnson (9)
Manford Primary School

The Portuguese Beach

You see the squawking seagulls sing sea songs,
The sea shines in the sunshine brightly.
Sandy sandcastles glisten in the sun.
This is the Portuguese beach at dawn.

Hear the whooshing waves *crash, smash* and *bash,*
Hear the footsteps crush the sparkly sand,
Chatting is all mums do.
This is the Portuguese beach at noon.

Touch the water and feel it gently drip off rocks,
Will tickle in-between your toes,
Touch the smooth shells as the waves wash them up,
This is the Portuguese beach in the evening.

Smell the salty seawater when you swim,
Smell the cold suncream on your arms and legs,
Smell the hot dogs and chips being served.
This is the Portuguese beach in late noon.

Taste the sand glowing in your mouth,
The water will roll into your mouth when you lay down,
Taste your cold milkshake when you drink it
This is the Portuguese beach at night.

Shaun McFarlane (9)
Manford Primary School

It's Like This In Portugal

Feel the whooshing waves,
Hitting the rocky, rocky sea and you,
Soft sand under your feet,
Making a crunching, munching noise.

Whooshing wind wafting in the air,
Rocks cracking as you walk
Bashing, crashing as the tide comes,
Whoosh, whoosh, goes the deep blue salty sea.

Smell the salty sea,
And the suncream on your body,
Chips, sausages and sand,
The smell wafts into the air.

Taste the salty seawater,
In your mouth it's horrible,
The sand tastes horrible,
While it's crunching in your mouth.

The tide you can see
And the boats go over it
See people paddling with fun
It's those days in Portugal.

Alexandra Elliott (9)
Manford Primary School

Portugal Is Like This

The sea is splashing and swirling,
The sand just stays there time and time,
The slippery, smooth pebbles are pink,
The swimming pool splashes roughly.

We can hear the chat of chattering people,
And roaring and racing of waves,
The squawking and squeaking of seagulls
And the sand rustling and rustling.

We can feel the sweat, squeezing our heads,
And cool and cold water,
And the wind whirling around,
The heat, hovering over our heads.

We can taste the soggy sand,
The sour and salty water,
The freezing and frosty drinks,
And the feasty, fabulous food.

We can smell the fragrance of flowers,
The fabulous smell of the food,
The light smell of the sand,
And the smell of swirling sea.

Rawal Butt (9)
Manford Primary School

Sea

The sea is like a swimming pool
The sea is like smooth sand
The sea is like sandcastles
The sea is like waves
I can hear waves whooshing
I can hear seagulls
I can hear sea swishing
I can hear talking
I feel hot
I can feel wind soft and hot
I can feel cold water
I can feel water coming up
I can taste sand
I can taste salty water
I can taste healthy water
I can smell suncream
I can smell sand
I can smell the sea
I can smell flowers.

Lareb Khan (8)
Manford Primary School

What's In Portugal?

The shimmering sea shines at the rock,
You can see the seagulls in the sky,
You can see the people playing in the sand,
You can see the palm trees swaying slowly.

> You can
> Hear the
> Seagulls
> Squawking
> And sand
> Crunching.
> You can
> Feel the
> Sand crunching
> Under your
> Feet and
> The cool
> Breezes.
> You can
> Taste the
> Sand
> Creeping in
> Your mouth.

You can smell the suncream, fish and salt,
You can smell the salty sea and the smell coming from across
the road.

That's what it's like in Portugal.

Milanda Khan (8)
Manford Primary School

It's Like This In Portugal

I can see boats beating in the sun.
I can see the shining sea.
I can see crabs crunching their claws.
I can see rocky rocks.

I can hear people talking,
I can hear a waft of food.
I can smell the food.
I can smell the salty sea.

I can taste the food melting.
I can taste the food.
I can taste the sand.
I can smell the salty sea.

I can smell seaweed.
I can hear talking.
I can see a lovely swimming pool.
I can feel the cold water.

I can see people eating food.
I can hear people walking in and out.
I can see kids playing.
I can see the big shining sun.

Louise Ambrose (9)
Manford Primary School

September

September is here
Back to school
Simple faces
Nothing at all
Some kids laughing
Some kids playing
Mainly working
Teachers smoking
Back to school
September is here
Simple faces
Nothing at all
Back to school forever.

Heather Everingham (9)
Manford Primary School

At The Beach What Do You See?

The shiny shimmery sea
Crashes and splashes
On the
Soft, crunching beach.

The spritely seagulls shout
But they aren't
So cute,
They just want your food.

The children shout and
Cry but they
Sometimes really
Are very shy.

The people sunbathing getting
Sunburnt in the scorching
Hot summer's sun.

Isha Kulkarni (9)
Manford Primary School

It's Like This

I can see water, I can see waves
I can touch the sand sitting by the sea
I can see the water in the swimming pool.

I can see lots of sandcastles on the floor
I can hear people sitting by the sea, talking
I can hear seagulls in the sea
I can hear the waves in the sea
I can hear the shiny sea foaming in the water.

I feel so hot, on my head, on the sea
I feel the cold when I get in the sea
I feel hot wind blowing at me
I feel the crunchy sandcastle beneath my feet.

I taste the salty water when it gets in my mouth
I taste the sand when my mouth opens.
I taste the healthy water when I open my mouth
I taste the sea coming towards me.

I smell sandcastles, the sea smothers my mouth
I smell the sand coming up my nose
I smell the lovely foam coming up my nose
I smell the suncream on my arms.

Tommy Edwards (9)
Manford Primary School

This Is Like Portugal

I can see whooshing waves glistening,
The smooth sand under my feet,
Seagulls enjoying their fly,
This is like Portugal.

I can hear children splashing in the water,
Waves crashing into the rugged rocks,
The salty sea whooshing as it sways,
This is like Portugal.

I can feel the smooth sand,
The cool breeze wafting in the air,
The hotness of the sunshine
This is like Portugal.

I can taste the salty sea,
The sand in my mouth,
The taste of ice cream
This is like Portugal.

I can smell the food wafting in the air,
The salty sea,
The suncream on your body,
This is like Portugal.

Neha Karthikeyan (9)
Manford Primary School

The Storm

It's a storm!
Children dying while parents sit crying.
The ship in the storm is banging and crashing.
The wind rages, roars, swirling and thundering.
The waves rage and roar and rumble.
The wrecked ship sinking and turning, while the wind damages
the ship.
The passengers climbing, some shouting, screaming and
even shaking.
The ship's turning and shaking, the wind is raging,
The waves are roaring,
The ship is getting damaged,
It's a storm!

Anna Clare (9)
Manford Primary School

Bouncy Hair

There's a boy with big hair.
His name is Jordan, he doesn't care.
He shakes it around, he doesn't care.
Now his hair is all cut off.
He feels sad but not bad.

Jordan Harry (9)
Manford Primary School

Barney

Please don't be mean or I will scream
Are you clean and do you wear hand cream?
Oh and have you seen a light beam?

The dog was on the boat and fell and rang a bell.
He saw a seashell, he swam back up and started to float.
He found a coat from off the boat.

Now I found out that the dog wears cream
And he fell in a stream.

The dog is light on his big night,
And it might give some people a fright,
On Barney's big night.

On Barney's big night there will be lots of light,
And the light is bright.

The dog is asleep now, so let's go to sleep now.
Now it's goodnight from Barney.

Amie Daniels Lydon (9)
Manford Primary School

In Portugal

I can see the salty sea,
Squawking seagulls flapping their wings hard,
A moulded mountain shone by the sun.
I am in Portugal.

I can hear the wet waves,
Jumping about talking.
People all around,
Bouncy boats on the sea,
I am in Portugal.

I can feel a gust of air, salt sea.
Swimming, a lot of heat,
Sitting on the beach,
I am in Portugal.

I can taste nice food here.
Fruity foods while enjoying myself.
Swimming, swallowing salt accidentally,
I am in Portugal.

I can smell flowers from the hotel
And delicious food there.
I smell flavoured water bottles.
I am in Portugal.

Tarrell Hinds (9)
Manford Primary School

My Rain Poem

Splash, the rain splashed down like snow.
Storm dripping, dropping, pitter-patter on windows.
Puddles go *splish, splash,* sploshing to the ground.
Getting umbrellas soaked by the sea.
Drops crashing to the ground, splashing, *splash, splash.*
No people out playing, rain is just pouring.
It is very boring, looking out of the windows.
Bored inside, they just want to play and not wait.
Puddles pitter-patter, people splashing in puddles.
Rainy, wet boots and rainjackets, hoods up, waterproof material.
Still can hear pitter-patter and *splish, splash, splosh.*
People still hear trickle, trickle on the roads.
Big splashes, the sound of moody children not liking the rain.
Dripping bus shelters, umbrellas up, hoods on.
People in puddles, *splish, splash* drop, *splosh.*

Melissa Clare (9)
Manford Primary School

There's A Monster in The Classroom

There's a monster in the classroom,
He's never having a laugh.
He sits on his chair moaning all day,
We never ignore him, not even for a single day.
If we do he'll play his awful didgeridoo.

Meanwhile, in the classroom he doesn't let us breathe!
So we make ourselves sneeze.
Would he like it if we treated him like he treats us?
Instead could we run him over with a bus?
So what shall we do?

Jesse Banister Wells (10)
Purleigh Primary School

Butterflies

B utterflies are small
U sually they are beautiful
T hey dance around high, with
T he sun in the sky
E veryone can see them
R ainbow-coloured like a gem
F lying round the nettles
L ooking for his friends
Y es! He's found them, now he can play!

Danielle Carruthers (11)
Purleigh Primary School

A Pocketful Of Rhyme

A rsene Wenger's red army makes the other teams look barmy

R eyes is so quick he helps Arsenal to be slick.

S ame old Arsenal, always scoring at the Lane.

E ngland stunned by the big guns.

N othing is going to stop Arsenal winning the Champions
League because they're all a bunch of dweebs.

A nything that is in our way is going in the trash because our
Way is the Wenger way.

L upoli is the best, better than the rest.

Taylor Burne (11)
Purleigh Primary School

Friends

Friends are all I have
They make me giggle and smile
They are my sunshine.

Above the white, cloudy sky
Where pretty birds fly
There they are, up very high.

Some are really shy
Some are crazy and funny
Most of them are mad.

They play with me all the time
We mostly play 'It'
Which makes us out of control.

I am the luckiest girl
To have many great friends
I'm as happy as can be.

Georgie Gefaell (11)
Purleigh Primary School

I Really Want A Mobile

I really want a mobile
I dream of them every day,
My mum says if I keep going on
She will take my money away.

I really want a mobile
I've been told I can't have one full stop.
And every time I go shopping
I stay away from the Vodaphone shop.

I really want a mobile
I think I'm turning mental,
Even my nan and grandad
Aren't being sentimental.

I really want a mobile
It's torture every day
I really want a mobile
To get this madness away.

George Dixon (11)
Purleigh Primary School

Yesterday, But The Day Before

Yesterday, but the day before,
Two tomcats came knocking at my door,
I opened the door to let them in,
And they knocked me down with a rolling pin.
The rolling pin was made of wood,
And I went flying on my hood.
I asked them around for a tasty tea,
With all their furry family,
And if they don't want to come,
I'll tickle their bums with a lump of celery!

Tyler Minot (11)
Purleigh Primary School

Snow

Snow is so cold
And you come and play
But wrap up warm
Or your hands will freeze
Now go and get a hot cup of hot chocolate now.

Snowflakes fall all day long,
Now let's go and build a snowman.
Oh for the fun we're having,
Wow, let's go before it snows.

Catherine Harvey (11)
Purleigh Primary School

Ferrari 430

Ha, you 430
I like it when you act dirty.
Doing some round those country lanes
And making smoke flare up behind you.
When you pull away every day
And then roar away.

When you change gear
I hear it when my dad drinks beer.
It's good to hear
I see the shine, here and there.
It makes me faint, when I see it
I could drive it quite a bit.

I love the colour of the badge
It makes me want to put it on my coat
And even on my boat.
I like the lovely 19" alloy wheels
I bet you get big bills
I want to get one.

Clarke Minot (11)
Purleigh Primary School

Sisters

S isters are boring, more like annoying
I hate sisters, they never share
S isters always smell like rotten eggs
T hey boss you about
E very time you say, 'Hi,' they just sit and look sly
R evolting rooms all dirty and dusty
S ister sly, sister smelly, all things are terrible with sisters.

Mason Kelly (11)
Purleigh Primary School

Arsenal

Football does rule
Even when you're in the pool
Arsenal play the best
Even though they're not from the west
Man U, give it a rest
You can't beat Arsenal, they're the best!
Stop having a try
We'll squish you like a fly.

Connor North (11)
Purleigh Primary School

I Saw A Stripy Cow

I saw a stripy cow
But I can't remember how.

If I see it again
I must be insane.

Is it really a stripy cow?
Or another creature, please tell me now.

Is there really a stripy cow?
'Ha, ha, ha,
No, son, it's called a zebra.'

Luke Seymour (11)
Purleigh Primary School

Snow

The cry of children playing in the snow
But there's one thing I don't know
Where and when the snowmen go?

The smell of hot chocolate steaming in the cup
And the pile of the wet soggy gloves going up, up, up.

That snow, oh that snow, a great white sheet
All compact and neat.

Weeee! I am sliding down the road now
On my great red sledge though
How am I going to stop?
I am laughing so much I think I might drop!

But the one thing I like the best
The laughter and the spirit of all the children playing
But now it's time to rest!

Annabel Baker (10)
Purleigh Primary School

The Sock

The steaming hot sock
Left to boil in the pan
As I am waiting by the clock,
It must have quite a tan!

Once I take it out the pan,
It still stinks really bad!
I must quickly put it in an empty can
Before my mum catches me being ever so mad!

I'd better soak it in fruit juice,
Then hopefully the smell will go
The threads have already gone loose
That means I will have to quickly sew.

The ingredients have gone right!
I have sown it all nice,
Now it's time to wear it in the shoe,
Oops! I forgot to do two!

James Sims (11)
Purleigh Primary School

The Best

Thierry Henry is cool
He didn't even go to school
Now he has got a 50-foot swimming pool
And at football he totally rules.

A rsenal
R ed
S uper
E xcellent
N ot beatable
A mazing goals
L ehmann.

Lloyd Jaques (11)
Purleigh Primary School

The Land In My Dreams

As I'm sitting downstairs my eyes are getting heavy
So I wander off to bed.
I climb up the ladder and lay down my head.
Suddenly I'm in a new world
How strange, my hair is curled.
Wow, look over there, there is a chocolate waterfall
Look out! A giant! How tall?

A beautiful rainbow, let's go find the gold
There's a leprechaun, he must be quite old.
I see fairies flying gracefully across the clear sky
I hear a soft voice, 'Everything's edible, have a try.'
Then I scoop up a handful of grass - oh tangy, appley, lemon, lime
I've been here ages, I wonder, *what is the time?*

This has been the best dream
Even better than the one where I was swimming in cream.
I think I should wake from this world
I don't really like my hair being curled.
I pinch myself, 1, 2, 3
I don't wake up, I'm stuck in this world, how can it be?

I finally wake, it's 7.30, I have to get ready for school
I can't wait to tell people my dream, it was a ball.

Christy Hill (11)
Purleigh Primary School

Daydreaming

As we're doing our times tables in maths,
I stare into space,
I'm in a different world,
I see a new place, I look up, the sky is green, everything is strange,
It's unbelievable to me!

Suddenly a man jumps out of a purple bush,
He's small and fat and gives me a push,
In a loud voice he greets my attention,
'Oi! Wake up young lady, that's an hour detention!'

I open my eyes, my teacher right in front of me,
I was in a faraway place, how can this be?
Then I remember, I'm not in a different land,
I'm still in my maths session,
My teacher sends me out,
That will teach me a lesson!

Hannah Ewart (11)
Purleigh Primary School

Space

S pace is big, too big to see
P lanets are like tiny peas
A n endless amount of stars
C ollecting around Mars
E ventually space will end.

T he spaceship will break and bend
H yperdriver will implode
E ach galaxy will explode.

F reaky aliens will survive
I n ugly beehives
N ebulae will disappear
A nts won't be in fear
L iving wormholes will hold.

F rightened ships with old
R ed lasers
O nly working weapons are phazers
N agging pirates destroying ships
T he ships blowing up into tiny bits
I ntellect turns to nothing
E ventually wormholes close, everything disappears
R everse time, this poem won't exist, but space will.

Charles Roffey (11)
Purleigh Primary School

Under My Bed

Under my bed I found
A man with no sound
Then I saw a man shouting, 'Help! I'm stuck.'
It turned out he was stuck down the loo, what a lout.
Then I saw a monster, it was green.
It looked mean.
That is all that is under my bed tonight.

Chavez Willson (11)
Purleigh Primary School